my True Girl Diary

DANNAH GRESH

MYTRUEGIRL.COM

Cover and interior design by Julia Ryan/DesignByJulia

Cover photo ©Shutterstock, BaLL LunLa

Interior spot illustrations by various Shutterstock artists.

TRUE GIRL is a registered trademark of Dannah Gresh.

MY TRUE GIRL© DIARY
Copyright © 2020 by Dannah Gresh
Published by Dannah Gresh / Pure Freedom Ministries
State College, PA 16801
www.dannahgresh.com

ISBN 978-1-7361015-0-6

Welcome to your very own
True Girl Diary!

This little book is *super special*. At first you
might notice that the pages seem blank. Look again!
These pages aren't empty—they are actually full
of *possibility*! Yes, what makes this book so
special is that it is written by YOU.

This diary is a treasure chest for you to
hide away your thoughts, hopes, prayers,
doodles, and more! It's a place for you
to collect your favorite Bible verses,
write your heart out to God, make lists
of what you're thankful for, or come up
with a brand new idea! You get to
decide what is kept in here.

This diary will keep it all safe,
so later you can come back and
remember all the wonderful things
you've discovered along the way!

Ready. Set. Write!
Dannah

MY FIRST TRUE GIRL DIARY ENTRY!

Dear Diary,

♥ My name is _____.

♥ I am _____ years old.

♥ My favorite thing to do is _____
_____
_____
_____.
_____

♥ I love to eat _____
_____.

♥ I am going to use this diary to _____

_____

_____

_____

_____

♥ My favorite Bible verse is _____

_____

_____

_____

_____

_____

_____

Love,

_____

(sign your name here!)

DOODLE!
NOODLE!
DOODLE!

DOODLE!
NOODLE!
DOODLE!

Jesus said to the people who believed in him, "You are truly my disciples if you remain faithful to my teachings. And you will know the truth, and the truth will set you free."

John 8:31-32

MY FAVE BIBLE VERSE TODAY!

SPACE FOR MY THOUGHTS

DOODLE!
NOODLE!
DOODLE!

DOODLE!
NOODLE!
DOODLE!

For we are God's masterpiece. He has
created us anew in Christ Jesus, so we can do
the good things he planned for us long ago.

Ephesians 2:10

MY FAVE BIBLE VERSE TODAY!

♥ WHAT I FEEL TODAY IS... ♥

. . . .

. . . .

. . . .

. . . .

. . . .

. . . .

. . . .

. . . .

. . . .

. . . .

. . . .

. . . .

DOODLE!
NOODLE!
DOODLE!

DOODLE!
NOODLE!
DOODLE!

. . . .

. . . .

. . . .

. . . .

. . . .

. . . .

. . . .

. . . .

. . . .

. . . .

. . . .

. . . .

. . . .

. . . .

I praise you because I am fearfully and wonderfully
made; your works are wonderful, I know that full well.

Psalm 139:14 (NIV)

MY FAVE BIBLE VERSE TODAY!

☆ I'M THINKING ABOUT... ☆

DOODLE!
NOODLE!
DOODLE!

DOODLE!
NOODLE!
DOODLE!

If I acted crazy, I did it for God; if I acted overly serious,
I did it for you. Christ's love has moved me to such extremes.
His love has the first and last word in everything we do.

2 Corinthians 5:13-14 (MSG)

MY FAVE BIBLE VERSE TODAY!

DEAR JESUS, THANKS FOR LISTENING!
I WANT YOU TO KNOW...

DOODLE!
NOODLE!
DOODLE!

DOODLE!
NOODLE!
DOODLE!

Walk with the wise and become wise,
for a companion of fools suffers harm.

Proverbs 13:20 (NIV)

MY FAVE BIBLE VERSE TODAY!

❀ THANK YOU, GOD, FOR... ❀

DOODLE!
NOODLE!
DOODLE!

DOODLE!
NOODLE!
DOODLE!

You are altogether beautiful, my love;
there is no flaw in you.

Song of Solomon 4:7 (NIV)

MY FAVORITE THINGS THIS WEEK ARE...

DOODLE!
NOODLE!
DOODLE!

DOODLE!
NOODLE!
DOODLE!

Don't worry about anything; instead, pray
about everything. Tell God what you need,
and thank him for all he has done.

Philippians 4:6

MY HIGH TODAY WAS...

MY LOW TODAY WAS...

(A "high" is the best thing that happened to you today!
A "low" is the biggest bummer of the day.)

DOODLE!
NOODLE!
DOODLE!

DOODLE!
NOODLE!
DOODLE!

The LORD is my strength and my shield; my heart
trusts in him, and he helps me. My heart leaps for
joy, and with my song I praise him.

Psalm 28:7 (NIV)

DEAR GOD, I AM GRATEFUL FOR...